A Guide to
AMERICAN STATES

Tennessee

THE VOLUNTEER STATE

MEDIA ENHANCED BOOKS

AV2
BY WEIGL

ADDED VALUE • AUDIO VISUAL

www.av2books.com

AV² provides enriched content that supplements and complements this book. Weigl's AV² books strive to create inspired learning and engage young minds in a total learning experience.

Your AV² Media Enhanced books come alive with...

Audio
Listen to sections of the book read aloud.

Key Words
Study vocabulary, and complete a matching word activity.

Video
Watch informative video clips.

Quizzes
Test your knowledge.

Embedded Weblinks
Gain additional information for research.

Slide Show
View images and captions, and prepare a presentation.

Try This!
Complete activities and hands-on experiments.

... and much, much more!

Go to **www.av2books.com**, and enter this book's unique code.

BOOK CODE

Y913164

AV² by Weigl brings you media enhanced books that support active learning.

Published by AV² by Weigl
350 5th Avenue, 59th Floor
New York, NY 10118
Website: www.av2books.com   www.weigl.com

Library of Congress Cataloging-in-Publication Data

Semchuk, Rosann.
 Tennessee / Rosann Semchuk.
    p. cm. -- (A guide to American states)
 Includes index.
 ISBN 978-1-61690-815-7 (hardcover : alk. paper) -- ISBN 978-1-61690-491-3 (online)
 1. Tennessee--Juvenile literature. I. Title.
 F436.3.S463 2011
 976.8--dc23
                              2011019034

Printed in the United States of America in North Mankato, Minnesota

052011
WEP180511

Project Coordinator Jordan McGill
Art Director Terry Paulhus

Photo Credits
Every reasonable effort has been made to trace ownership and to obtain permission to reprint copyright material. The publishers would be pleased to have any errors or omissions brought to their attention so that they may be corrected in subsequent printings.

Weigl acknowledges Getty Images as its primary image supplier for this title.

Contents

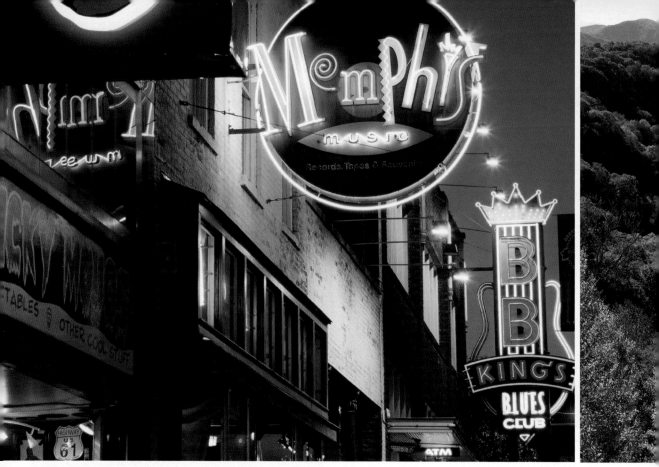

Colorful Beale Street in downtown Memphis is lined with blues clubs, restaurants, and shops.

Introduction

If you have an ear for blues music, Tennessee is the place to visit. Memphis, the most populous city in Tennessee, was an important location during the blues craze that occurred in the United States during the early 1900s. Beale Street was Memphis' main music district, made famous by blues composer W. C. Handy. Known as the Father of the Blues, Handy released his first hit song, "Memphis Blues," in 1912. The blues, a style of African American folk music, was relatively unknown to many people in the United States. Handy's songs and Beale Street brought these soulful tunes into the limelight. Memphis is mentioned in many other popular songs, too.

Great Smoky Mountains National Park receives more visitors than any other national park in the United States.

Tennessee's capital, Nashville, is a center for the country music industry.

The name Tennessee also brings to mind the songs of Elvis Presley and Nashville country music, as well as the Great Smoky Mountains, frontiersman Davy Crockett, President Andrew Jackson, and the Civil War.

A large portion of Tennessee is **rural**, and the state's economy was, until recently, largely based on agriculture. Although some Tennesseans still work on farms, most people work in such locations as offices, retail outlets, and factories. Tennessee became more **industrialized** during the 20th century. The state's largest shift toward industrialization occurred in the 1930s with the development of the Tennessee River basin under the Tennessee Valley Authority, or TVA. The TVA's programs attracted a number of different industries, including the federal government's atomic energy program at what became the Oak Ridge National Laboratory.

Where Is Tennessee?

Tennessee has more than 87,000 miles of highways and roads. The main highway in Tennessee is Interstate 40, an east-west route that links the state's main cities. Major highways that run north-south include Interstates 24, 65, and 75. The key transportation centers in Tennessee are Memphis, Nashville, Knoxville, and Chattanooga. Barges navigate the Tennessee River, but the state's main port is on the Mississippi River, near Memphis.

Memphis International Airport is the "SuperHub" for FedEx Express. Because of this, the airport is the world's largest air cargo handler.

The name Tennessee attests to the historical significance of American Indians in the state. "Tennessee" is derived from a Cherokee word, Tanase. The exact meaning of the word isn't known, but it may have meant "winding river." Tanase was a Cherokee town. It was situated on the banks of the Tennessee River, a river that bends to such an extent that it flows through the state twice.

Over the years Tennessee has been given several nicknames, but the most popular is the Volunteer State. The nickname originated during the War of 1812 against the British. Many brave volunteer soldiers from Tennessee fought in the battle of New Orleans under General Andrew Jackson. This battle marked the beginning of Tennessee's great military tradition.

Tennessee is often considered a divider state between the North and the South. During the Civil War, Tennessee's loyalties were divided as well. Tennessee was the last state to leave the Union and the first to return.

I DIDN'T KNOW THAT!

Tennessee is divided into 95 counties.

Nashville's original name was Nashborough.

Until the 1940s, farming was the most important economic activity in the state.

The Tennessee River is more than 650 miles long. It is an important shipping route and provides water for crops and to produce electricity.

Mapping
Tennessee

Tennessee is bounded by the Appalachian Mountains on the east and the Mississippi River on the west. The Great Smoky Mountains are part of the Appalachian chain. Tennessee shares its borders with eight other states. Kentucky and Virginia lie to the north. North Carolina borders Tennessee to the east. Georgia, Alabama, and Mississippi lie to the south, and Arkansas and Missouri border the state to the west.

Sites and Symbols

STATE SEAL
Tennessee

STATE BIRD
Mockingbird

STATE FLOWER
Iris

STATE FLAG
Tennessee

STATE FRUIT
Tomato

STATE TREE
Tulip poplar

Nickname The Volunteer State

Motto Agriculture and Commerce

Song "My Homeland Tennessee," words by Nell Grayson Taylor and music by Roy Lamont Smith

Entered the Union June 1, 1796, as the 16th state

Capital Nashville

Population (2010 Census) 6,346,105 Ranked 17th State

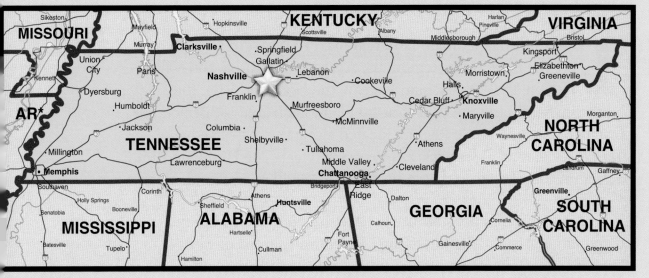

*Arkansas

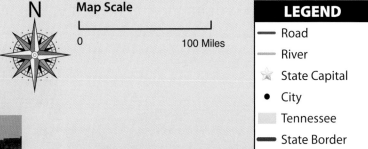

N

Map Scale

0   100 Miles

LEGEND
— Road
— River
⭐ State Capital
• City
▢ Tennessee
— State Border

United States

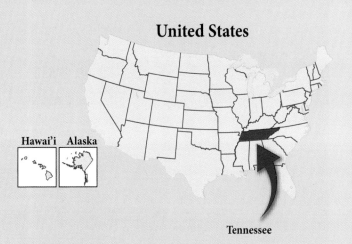

Hawai'i   Alaska

Tennessee

STATE CAPITAL

Nashville is Tennessee's capital and second-largest city. Since 1963, the government of Nashville has been consolidated with that of Davidson County, in which the city is located. In the course of the state's history, three other cities served as its capital before Nashville. These cities are Kingston, Murfreesboro, and Knoxville. Nashville is considered to be the center of the country music industry. It is nicknamed "Music City."

The Land

Tennessee has six main land regions. From east to west, they are the Blue Ridge Region, the Appalachian Ridge and Valley Region, the Appalachian Plateau, the Highland Rim, the Nashville Basin, and the Gulf Coastal Plain. Each area is distinct. For instance, the Blue Ridge Region, located along the eastern edge of Tennessee, has an average elevation of 5,000 feet. The Highland Rim is a generally level plateau that is cut by many small ravines and streams.

The largest rivers in the state are the Mississippi, Tennessee, and Cumberland rivers. The Mississippi River drains most of west Tennessee. Its largest **tributaries** in the state include the Forked Deer, Hatchie, Loosahatchie, Obion, and Wolf rivers. The Tennessee and Cumberland rivers drain most of the rest of the state.

CLINGMAN'S DOME

Clingman's Dome, located in the Blue Ridge Region, is the state's highest peak. It rises to 6,643 feet.

REELFOOT LAKE

Reelfoot Lake, in the northwestern part of the state, is Tennessee's largest natural lake. It is a popular spot for fishing, hiking, and bird watching.

FALL CREEK FALLS

With a drop of 256 feet, Fall Creek Falls is the tallest free-fall waterfall east of the Mississippi River. It is located in Fall Creek Falls State Park.

TENNESSEE RIVER GORGE

The Tennessee River Gorge, west of Chattanooga, winds through the southern Cumberland Mountains. It is home to more than 1,000 different types of plants

I DIDN'T KNOW THAT!

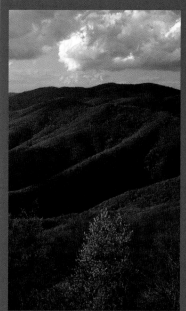

Some scientists believe that the many pine trees in the Great Smoky Mountains release a chemical that contributes to the hazy appearance of the range.

Tennessee measures 432 miles across at its widest east-west point and 112 miles at its longest point from north to south.

Tennessee has 926 square miles of inland water.

Most of Tennessee's lakes are human made.

Tennessee's summers can be very hot. The state receives the majority of its rainfall in winter and early spring.

Climate

Most of Tennessee has a humid, subtropical climate. Typically, temperatures rarely rise above 100° Fahrenheit or fall below 10° F. Tennessee's summers are hot, but residents are rewarded with mild winters. Snowfall is light in the central and western parts of the state, but it is often heavy in the eastern mountains. The hottest temperature ever recorded in the state was 113° F in Perryville, on two different dates in 1930. The coldest is −32° F, recorded on December 30, 1917 in Mountain City.

Average July Temperatures Across Tennessee

Temperatures in most parts of Tennessee are warm in the summer, and many people think it feels even hotter because of the humidity. Some areas are warmer than others. What factors might make the average July temperature higher in Memphis than in Mountain City?

Degrees Fahrenheit

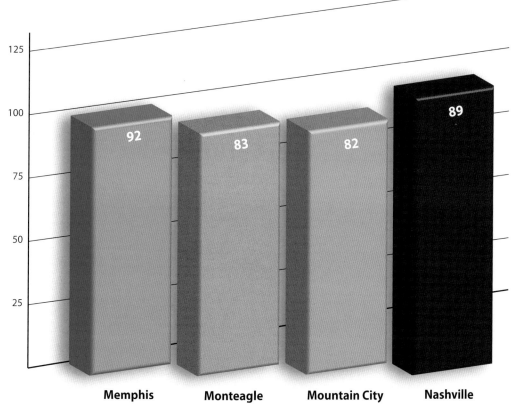

Memphis	Monteagle	Mountain City	Nashville
92	83	82	89

Natural Resources

Tennessee has fertile soils, a vast supply of water, and an abundance of minerals. Some of the state's most fertile soils are found in the Appalachian Ridge and Valley Region and in the Nashville Basin. Fertile soils consisting of sand, silt, and clay also cover the Gulf Coastal Plain. The Appalachian Plateau and much of the Highland Rim, however, have poor-quality soils.

There are 15 state forests in Tennessee. The resources in these forests are carefully protected.

Beneath the soil are many valuable minerals. In the east there are large deposits of marble, pyrite, and zinc. In central Tennessee limestone and zinc are found. Coal deposits can be found around the Appalachian Plateau.

Forestry is another economic activity that depends on Tennessee's natural resources. There are almost 14 million acres of forest land in the state. Tennessee is one of the leading producers of hardwood lumber among all U.S. states.

Many companies in Tennessee extract sand and gravel from pits called quarries.

Limestone, which is found in large amounts in Tennessee, was declared the official state rock in 1979.

The Tennessee Valley Authority is a major producer of **hydroelectricity**, which is generated when flowing water spins turbines at the TVA's many dams.

Crushed stone, zinc, cement, sand, gravel, and clay are common minerals found in Tennessee.

Tennessee ranks first in the nation in the production of hardwood flooring and pencils.

Plants

More than half of Tennessee is forested. This is a significant improvement since the 1920s, when only about one-third of the state was forested. The regrowth of Tennessee forests is due to reforestation, the deliberate replanting of trees. Hardwoods make up most of the state's trees. The most common tree species are soft maple, white oak, hickory, red cedar, and blackgum, also called tupelo. The forests of eastern Tennessee include red spruce and Fraser fir trees, while western Tennessee forests include black willow, cottonwood, and silver maple.

The bald cypress is common in the low, swampy bottomlands of western Tennessee. Big Cypress Tree State Park was once home to the largest and oldest bald cypress tree in the United States. This cone-bearing hardwood was 175 feet tall and 40 feet in **circumference**. Unfortunately the tree was struck by lightning in 1976, ending its life after 1,350 years.

BALD CYPRESS

Cypress trees in swampy areas often have wide, swollen trunks. These trunks are called buttresses.

PASSIONFLOWER

Tennessee's state wildflower, the passionflower, was called the ocoee by the state's Cherokee Indians. The Ocoee Valley and Ocoee River are named for the flower.

LIGHT BLUE CHICORY

Light blue chicory, a flower commonly found in the eastern part of the state, is edible.

IRIS

Tennessee's state flower was once prized as an important perfume ingredient. Irises can be found throughout the state.

Shrubs and flowering trees in the state include dogwoods, red flame azaleas, and rhododendrons.

Tennessee's state tree, the tulip poplar, is not actually a poplar. It is a member of the magnolia family.

The American chestnut tree was almost wiped out by disease in the 1930s. Two of the largest trees surviving today are in Jackson County.

The trumpet-shaped Indian Pink can be found in limestone soils in the Great Smoky Mountains.

Animals

Tennessee is home to a **diverse** animal population. Black bears roam remote parts of the state's Great Smoky Mountains. These bears are considered symbols of Great Smoky Mountains National Park, which for them is a protected habitat. Thanks to protection from hunting and loss of habitat, black bear populations rose dramatically in the late 20th century. When they are tracking prey, black bears can run as fast as 35 miles per hour. They are also skilled tree climbers.

Small mammals are abundant in Tennessee and include beavers, muskrats, rabbits, raccoons, skunks, and squirrels. The flying squirrel is the smallest type of tree squirrel. This tiny animal is mostly **nocturnal**. It has a fold of skin that stretches from its front leg to its rear leg on both sides of its body. When a flying squirrel stretches out its legs, the folds of skin become taut and form "wings." This excess skin allows the squirrel to glide for distances of up to 150 feet.

TENNESSEE CAVE SALAMANDER

The Tennessee cave salamander is the state reptile. It is most commonly found in limestone caves in the southern and central parts of the state.

BEAVER

Beavers can be found building dams and homes called lodges throughout Tennessee. The animals usually sleep during the day and do their work at night.

SOUTHERN COPPERHEAD

Tennessee is home to poisonous snakes, including the southern copperhead. These copperheads are found in the southwestern part of the state.

RACCOON

Tennessee's state animal, the raccoon, was once aggressively hunted for its fur. The raccoon has now made a comeback and can be found throughout the state, in both rural and urban areas.

Tennessee has two official state insects. They are the ladybug and the firefly.

The Mississippi Flyway, in the western portion of the state, is used by millions of birds as a migratory route, as they travel south for the winter and back north in the spring.

Fish found in Tennessee include black bass, carp, perch, and catfish.

The state gem is the river pearl, which is found in the shells of freshwater mussels. River pearls come in various shapes and colors.

The Eastern box turtle is Tennessee's state reptile.

Tourism

Every year millions of tourists go to Tennessee with music on their minds. Nashville and Memphis draw many visitors interested in discovering the state's musical heritage. Elvis Presley's home in Memphis is preserved as a museum. He lived on a 14-acre estate called Graceland. Today visitors can tour the lavish mansion. The highlight of the mansion tour is Elvis's trophy room, which holds his gold records, awards, and career mementos.

On a different musical note is Nashville, home of the Grand Ole Opry. This live country-music show has hosted talented country performers since 1925. Today the Grand Ole Opry features contemporary and traditional country-music performances. Featured performers in 2011 included Carrie Underwood, Blake Shelton, and the Charlie Daniels Band.

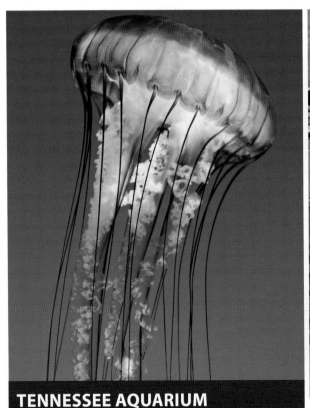

TENNESSEE AQUARIUM

The Tennessee Aquarium in Chattanooga is the world's largest freshwater aquarium. It contains more than 10,000 animal species.

GREAT SMOKY MOUNTAINS NATIONAL PARK

Great Smoky Mountains National Park covers more than 800 square miles. One of its popular attractions is the observation tower at Clingmans Dome.

GRACELAND

Graceland, the estate of Elvis Presley, features a 23-room mansion. It is one of the most visited buildings in the United States.

DOLLYWOOD

Country superstar Dolly Parton, from Locust Ridge, never forgot her Tennessee roots. Her theme park, Dollywood, is nestled near Great Smoky Mountains National Park. The park features music, crafts, attractions, and rides.

Industry

A griculture is a vital industry in Tennessee's economy. Two of the state's leading crops are soybeans and corn. Other common crops grown in the state include cotton, strawberries, and tobacco. In eastern Tennessee there are many livestock farms. Livestock farmers raise a variety of animals, including cattle, hogs, chickens, and sheep. Beef cattle are the leading source of income in the livestock industry. There are more than 2 million head of cattle in the state.

Industries in Tennessee
Value of Goods and Services in Millions of Dollars

Service industries are a major part of the Tennessee's economy. People in service industries work in places visited by tourists, as well as in such places as schools, hospitals, and government offices. What are some of the kinds of services that people in the tourism industry provide?

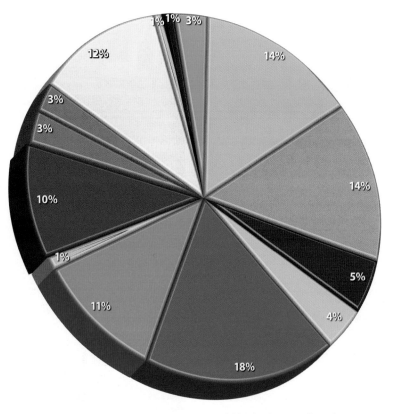

LEGEND

	Agriculture, Forestry, and Fishing	$1,400
*	Mining	$264
	Utilities	$1,749
	Construction	$8,088
	Manufacturing	$34,897
	Wholesale and Retail Trade	$34,273
	Transportation	$11,592
	Media and Entertainment	$10,877
	Finance, Insurance, and Real Estate	$43,686
	Professional and Technical Services	$27,635
	Education	$2,336
	Health Care	$23,359
	Hotels and Restaurants	$8,433
	Other Services	$7,691
	Government	$28,228
	TOTAL	**$244,508**

*Less than 1%. Percentages may not add to 100 because of rounding.

Tennessee's main manufactured products are chemicals, transportation equipment, processed foods and beverages, and machinery. Among the leading employers are Eastman Chemical, Nissan Motor Manufacturing Corporation, and McKee Foods Corporation. Located in Collegedale, McKee Foods is best-known for its Little Debbie® snack products.

Farms can be found throughout the Sequatchie Valley in the central part of the state.

The Mississippi River is the nation's chief inland waterway. It is spanned by the Hernando de Soto Bridge in Memphis.

Tomatoes and snap beans are among the most important vegetables grown in the state.

Tennessee farmers produce more than 320 million eggs every year.

Goods and Services

I n 1933 the Tennessee Valley Authority was created to develop the natural resources of the area and to provide jobs for workers in the region. The TVA built dams and harnessed waterpower to create electricity. Over the years the TVA has contributed greatly to Tennessee's prosperity and to its transition from an agricultural to an industrial-based economy. The TVA also manages coal-burning power plants. It manages 21 reservoir systems and is responsible for 175,000 acres of land near the reservoirs.

The TVA headquarters are in Knoxville. Power generated by the TVA is distributed over an area of about 80,000 square miles, serving a population of 8.5 million people. This area includes most of Tennessee and parts of Alabama, Virginia, Georgia, Kentucky, North Carolina, and Mississippi. The TVA produces more power than any other power system in the nation.

The Tennessee Valley Authority has been one of the state's largest employers since the 1930s.

Nearly 26,000 students attend the University of Tennessee in Knoxville.

Community, business, and personal services are the most important parts of Tennessee's service sector. FedEx Corporation, a company that specializes in package delivery and information technology, has a large base in Memphis. It is one of the state's largest private employers. Tourism and retail businesses are leading sources of employment throughout the state. The state government also employs many Tennesseans.

Other economic activities in the service sector include health care and education. Johnson City, Memphis, and Nashville are important health centers in Tennessee. Each has large hospitals and colleges of medicine. Tennessee has several major universities. They include the University of Tennessee, Middle Tennessee State University, the University of Memphis, Vanderbilt University, Fisk University, and Tennessee State University.

American Indians

People have been living in Tennessee for at least 11,000 years. About 2,000 years ago, people of the Woodland culture grew crops, made clay pottery, and built mounds. Most of these mounds were used for burials, and some can still be seen throughout the state. More recently, American Indian groups that have called Tennessee home include the Cherokee, the Chickasaw, and the Yuchi, all of whom settled along the banks of Tennessee's major rivers. The Cherokee and the Chickasaw were the most powerful groups. The Cherokee lived and hunted in eastern Tennessee, near the upper area of the Tennessee River, and the Chickasaw inhabited western Tennessee. Both groups claimed the middle portion of the state and clashed over this territory until the 1800s.

The Sequoyah Birthplace Museum in Vonore is dedicated to the history and culture of the Cherokee people.

Spanish explorers were the first Europeans to reach Tennessee. Their arrival had unfortunate consequences, as they introduced new diseases that killed many American Indians. By the time the French entered Tennessee in the late 1600s, the American Indian population had been greatly reduced.

Hernando de Soto made many important discoveries in Tennessee, but he and his men killed many American Indians during their travels.

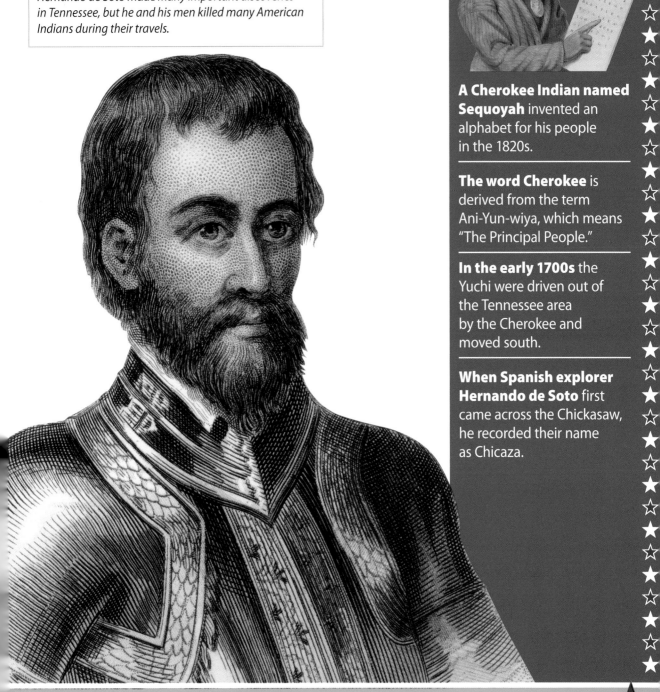

A Cherokee Indian named Sequoyah invented an alphabet for his people in the 1820s.

The word Cherokee is derived from the term Ani-Yun-wiya, which means "The Principal People."

In the early 1700s the Yuchi were driven out of the Tennessee area by the Cherokee and moved south.

When Spanish explorer Hernando de Soto first came across the Chickasaw, he recorded their name as Chicaza.

Spanish explorer Juan Pardo built forts in Tennessee and several other states.

Explorers

Hernando de Soto led the first Spanish explorers into the Tennessee area. This group reached the valley of the Tennessee River in 1540. De Soto then traveled farther west and became the first European to reach the Mississippi River. He crossed the river in 1541, near the site of present-day Memphis. Spaniard Juan Pardo explored eastern Tennessee in the 1560s and built several forts in the area, including one near what is now Chattanooga. The Spanish presence in the region was never extensive, however.

More than a century later, in 1682, French explorer René-Robert Cavelier, sieur de La Salle, claimed the entire Mississippi Valley for France. He built a trading post, Fort Prud'homme, on the Chickasaw Bluffs. The post was quickly abandoned due to its isolated location. In 1715 another French trading post, French Lick, was erected near the site of present-day Nashville. In 1763, Great Britain won control of what is now Tennessee after defeating France in the French and Indian War. The Treaty of Paris surrendered France's claims to almost all of its land east of the Mississippi.

Timeline of Settlement

Early Exploration

1540 Hernando de Soto is the first European to reach Tennessee.

1673 British fur trader Abraham Wood sends two men to East Tennessee to establish trading relations with the Cherokee Indians.

1682 La Salle explores the Mississippi Valley and claims it for France.

British Control

1754-1763 Britain and France fight the French and Indian War. The victory by the British brings what is now Tennessee under their control.

1763 The British government establishes the Proclamation Line, which runs across the top of the Appalachian Mountains, and tells settlers in its eastern North American colonies not go west of the line.

1772 The Watauga Association, formed by a group of settlers, writes its own constitution.

Road to Independence

1775 The American Revolution begins.

1783 The American colonies officially gain their independence from Britain. What is now Tennessee becomes part of the United States.

1784 The state of Franklin is formed by a group of settlers in eastern Tennessee. The U.S. government does not accept the new state.

Statehood and Civil War

1790 The U.S. Congress forms the Southwest Territory, which consists largely of the land that will become the state of Tennessee.

1796 Tennessee becomes the 16th state on June 1.

1861 Tennessee secedes from, or leaves, the Union and joins the Confederacy at the beginning of the Civil War.

1865 The Civil War ends with the defeat of the Confederacy.

1866 Tennessee reenters the Union as a state.

Early Settlers

I n 1763, the British king banned settlers in the American colonies from living in most parts of Tennessee. Most early settlers simply ignored the ban, however. People came to the area from nearby colonies such as Virginia and North Carolina. By 1769 hundreds of people were living in log cabins along the Watauga River Valley. At this time, many settlers still called themselves North Carolinians.

Map of Settlements and Resources in Early Tennessee

① *Spanish explorer Juan Pardo builds a fort near what is now Chattanooga in the 1560s.*

④ *French-Canadian Timothy Demonbreun builds a cabin near what is now Nashville in 1769 to use as a base for fur trading. His business becomes very successful.*

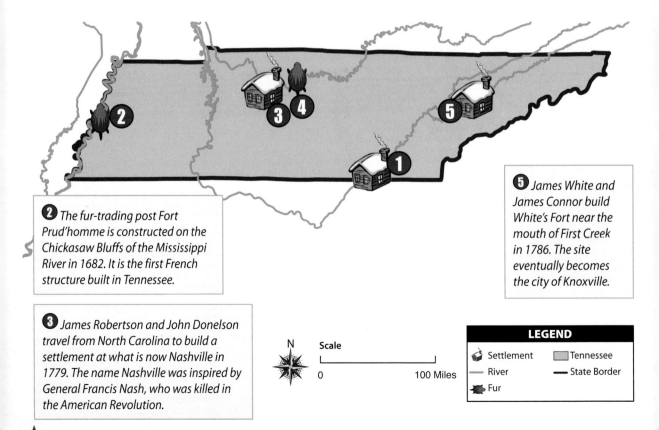

② *The fur-trading post Fort Prud'homme is constructed on the Chickasaw Bluffs of the Mississippi River in 1682. It is the first French structure built in Tennessee.*

⑤ *James White and James Connor build White's Fort near the mouth of First Creek in 1786. The site eventually becomes the city of Knoxville.*

③ *James Robertson and John Donelson travel from North Carolina to build a settlement at what is now Nashville in 1779. The name Nashville was inspired by General Francis Nash, who was killed in the American Revolution.*

N
Scale
0   100 Miles

LEGEND

Settlement		Tennessee	
River		State Border	
Fur			

In 1772 a group of settlers formed their own government called the Watauga Association. They drew up the first written constitution west of the Appalachians. Three years later a group called the Transylvania Company bought a large section of what is now Tennessee and Kentucky from the Cherokee. The Transylvania Company hired a highly regarded pioneer, Daniel Boone, to blaze a trail so that land could be opened to settlers. Boone's trail, named the Wilderness Road, served as the main route for new American settlers.

Many Tennessee settlers supported independence from Britain and fought in the American Revolution. In 1784, after the war, North Carolina gave up its claim to the Tennessee region. The U.S. Congress, however, declined to admit Tennessee into the Union at that time. About 10 years later, the people of the area proved that they had a population of 60,000, which was the requirement for statehood. In 1796, Tennessee adopted a state constitution, chose a governor, and elected Andrew Jackson to Congress. On June 1, 1796, Tennessee became the 16th state to join the United States.

The Chickasaw controlled nearly all of western Tennessee. In 1818, however, the Chickasaw **ceded** most of their land to the government. The Cherokee held on to a large tract of land in central Tennessee but were eventually forced off of most of their land by increased settlement.

Daniel Boone's Wilderness Road was used by settlers for more than 50 years.

Notable People

Many notable people from Tennessee have contributed to the development of their state and country. These people have included a U.S. president and other political leaders, military heroes, and women of achievement who broke barriers.

ANDREW JACKSON
(1767-1845)

Andrew Jackson was Tennessee's first congressman. He also served as a U.S. senator and state supreme court judge. As a commander in the War of 1812, he was given the nickname "Old Hickory" because he was so tough. He became a hero nationwide after he led the American forces to victory over the British in January 1815 at the Battle of New Orleans, the last major battle of the war. Jackson was elected president in 1828 and served two terms.

DAVY CROCKETT
(1786-1836)

Davy Crockett was one of Tennessee's best-known early settlers. Born in Greene County in 1786, Crockett was a pioneer and a politician. In 1826 he was elected to the U.S. House of Representatives. After he left Congress, Crockett went to Texas, where he fought on the side of the Texans in their war for independence from Mexico. While fighting for Texas, Crockett died at the Battle of the Alamo in 1836.

ALVIN YORK
(1887–1964)

Alvin York, born in Pall Mall, was one of World War I's most decorated soldiers. He was awarded the Medal of Honor for his service in the war. In total, York captured 132 enemy soldiers. After the war, he returned to Tennessee and founded a high school. His story was told in the 1941 movie *Sergeant York*.

WILMA RUDOLPH
(1940-1994)

Clarksville native Wilma Rudolph was born prematurely and suffered from the disease polio as a child. Polio left her with a twisted leg, but she still loved to play basketball and run. She competed in the Olympics in 1960 and won three gold medals in track and field events. She created Clarksville's first integrated event when she insisted that both blacks and whites attend her victory parade.

AL GORE
(1948–)

Albert Arnold Gore, Jr., was elected to the U.S. House of Representatives and then the U.S. Senate. He served as the 45th vice president of the United States from 1993 to 2001. Gore ran for president in 2000 but lost. In 2007 he won the Nobel Peace Prize for his environmental work.

I DIDN'T KNOW THAT!

Hattie Caraway (1878–1950), who was born near Bakerville, worked as a teacher in Tennessee. After she and her husband, Thaddeus, moved to Arkansas, he was elected to the U.S. Senate. When he died in 1931, she was temporarily appointed in her husband's place. She then won a special election to keep the seat for the remainder of the term. This made her the first woman elected to the Senate.

John Luther "Casey" Jones (1864-1900) was born in Jackson and worked as a railroad engineer. In 1900, Casey Jones was driving a train full of passengers from Memphis when he realized a freight train was blocking his way. Jones was able to slow the train down enough to save the lives of his passengers. He was the only person killed in the collision. Today, the Casey Jones Home and Railroad Museum is a popular Memphis attraction.

Population

I n 2010, Tennessee had a population of about 6.3 million people. Between 2000 and 2010, the state's population grew by 11.5 percent, which was higher than the national average of 9.7 percent. Tennessee is more densely populated than many parts of the nation. The average number of people per square mile in the United States is a little over 87, but in Tennessee the average is about 154 people per square mile.

Tennessee Population 1950–2010

Tennessee's population grew by more than 650,000 people between 2000 and 2010. What are some factors that might contribute to the state's rapid population growth?

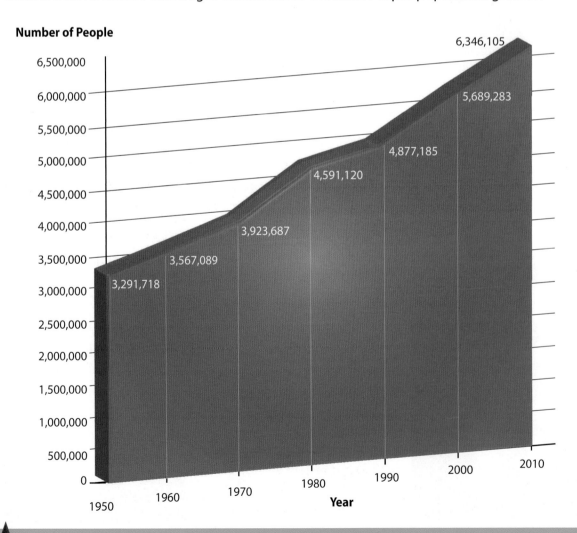

Number of People

Year	Population
1950	3,291,718
1960	3,567,089
1970	3,923,687
1980	4,591,120
1990	4,877,185
2000	5,689,283
2010	6,346,105

Year

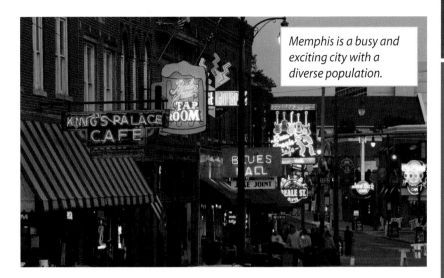
Memphis is a busy and exciting city with a diverse population.

The most populous city in the state is Memphis, with more than 675,000 people. Memphis covers an area of 256 square miles in the southwestern part of the state. African Americans make up more than half of the city's residents.

About 24 percent of the population of Tennessee is below the age of 18 years. Residents 65 years of age or older make up slightly more than 13 percent of the population. Both of these figures are close to the national averages.

The City of Murfreesboro lies in the exact geographic center of the state.

Many of Tennessee's residents live in small towns and rural areas.

Politics and Government

The governor of Tennessee is the head of the executive branch and serves a four-year term. The state legislature, called the General Assembly, has two chambers, or parts. They are a 33-member Senate and a 99-member House of Representatives.

The Tennessee State Capitol was completed in 1859. It is open to the public for tours.

Senators serve four-year terms, and House members are elected for two-year terms. Representatives must be at least twenty-one years old, and senators must be at least thirty. They are required to be U.S. citizens who have lived in the state for at least three years.

The highest court in Tennessee is the state Supreme Court, which consists of five justices elected for eight-year terms. Most of Tennessee's 95 counties are governed by county courts composed of elected justices of the peace. There are more than 340 **municipalities** in Tennessee, most of which are governed by a mayor and council.

Bill Haslam was elected governor of Tennessee in November 2010. A native of Knoxville, he served as that city's mayor before becoming governor.

I DIDN'T KNOW THAT!

Tennessee's state song is called "My Homeland, Tennessee."

Here is an excerpt from the song:

*O Tennessee, that gave
    us birth,
To thee our hearts bow down.
For thee our love and loyalty
Shall weave a fadeless crown.
Thy purple hills our
    cradle was;
Thy fields our mother breast
Beneath thy sunny
    bended skies,
Our childhood days
    were blessed.
Could we forget our heritage
Of heroes strong and brave?
Could we do aught
    but cherish it,
Unsullied to the grave?*

*Ah no! the State where
    Jackson sleeps,
Shall ever peerless be.
We glory in thy majesty;
Our homeland, Tennessee.*

Cultural Groups

African Americans have made significant contributions to Tennessee's culture. With African Americans making up more than half of Memphis' population, the city is a center of African American history and heritage. In Tennessee's early days, Memphis operated as a cotton and slave market. Later, in the mid-1900s, Memphis was central to the **civil rights movement**. Civil rights leader Dr. Martin Luther King Jr., was **assassinated** in Memphis in 1968. He is honored today at the National Civil Rights Museum. Located in Memphis, this museum provides an overview of the civil rights movement through its collections, exhibitions, and educational programs.

Tennessee's first African American millionaire, Robert R. Church, lived in Memphis. Church was born into slavery but went on to become a very successful businessman and community leader. In the late 1800s he helped the city of Memphis during a period of economic hardship by investing in city bonds.

The motel where Dr. Martin Luther King Jr. was assassinated is now the National Civil Rights Museum. A wreath marks the place where he was standing when he was shot.

The CMA Music Festival is held in Nashville every June. Featured performers have included Taylor Swift, Brad Paisley, and Keith Urban.

Tennessee hosts many festivals that honor and preserve the state's traditional Southern culture. Since its beginning in a little schoolhouse in 1926, the Appalachian Fair has grown in scope and attendance. Celebrating Tennessee's Southern and country-music traditions, the Appalachian Fair, held in Gray, offers a variety of entertainment every August. Today more than 220,000 people attend the fair annually. In recent years the main stage has welcomed entertainers such as Danny Gokey and The Band Perry.

The Memphis in May International Festival is a month-long celebration of local culture and cuisine. Memphis in May includes the Beale Street Music Festival, the World Championship Barbecue Cooking Contest, and the Great Southern Food Festival.

Arts and Entertainment

Early Tennessee traditions continue to influence the state's arts and entertainment scenes. Music and Southern folk culture are alive throughout the state. Bluegrass music has long been a rural Tennessee tradition, and blues music also has close ties to the state. African Americans have greatly influenced the Memphis music scene, and the city is widely known as the Home of the Blues. Music legends such as B. B. King helped to develop the Memphis blues style. Beale Street in Memphis was, and continues to be, the hub of blues, jazz, and soul music.

Memphis blues and gospel music greatly influenced Elvis Presley's musical style. Elvis moved to Memphis with his family at the age of 13. In 1954 he began his sensational singing career with the Sun Records label in Memphis. He died at his Memphis home, Graceland, on August 16, 1977. Today the Graceland mansion lures Elvis fans to Tennessee by the millions.

As well as being a talented singer, Elvis Presley starred in more than 30 Hollywood films.

Carrie Underwood has been a member of the Grand Ole Opry in Nashville since 2008. The Opry is the longest-running live radio program in the world.

Many celebrities and entertainers were born in the Volunteer State. Singer Aretha Franklin and actor Morgan Freeman were both born in Memphis. Franklin began singing in church at an early age and recorded her first album at the age of 14. She has since recorded many soul-music albums and is perhaps best known for her song "Respect." Freeman won an Academy Award in 2005 for his performance in *Million Dollar Baby*. In recent years he has played Lucius Fox alongside Christian Bale's Batman in the Dark Knight series.

For young people who enjoy the theater scene, the Nashville Children's Theater is the place to be. It began providing children's entertainment in the 1930s and continues to thrill thousands of children every year with its energetic performances.

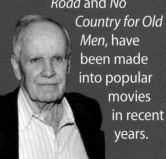

Sports

Tennessee is a playground for people who enjoy the outdoors. Residents can go mountain biking, hiking, and horseback riding. Water sports, such as fishing and swimming, are also popular. Tennessee boasts more than 20 major lakes and reservoirs and more than 19,000 miles of streams. Tennessee's official sport fish, the largemouth bass, is one of the most sought-after fish in the state. Its popularity with fishers is due to its strong fighting ability and large size.

Great Smoky Mountains National Park is a popular destination for outdoor enthusiasts. Visitors come to the park to hike, bike, camp, and go horseback riding. The Paris Landing State Resort Park is located on the Cumberland Plateau. Spelunkers, or cavers, head to this park to explore the many intricate caves in the area. Tennessee has more than 3,800 known caves.

Automobile racing is a great spectator sport in Tennessee. The Bristol Motor Speedway has earned a reputation as the World's Fastest Half-Mile. Darrell Waltrip, a resident of Tennessee, is Bristol's most successful racer of all time. Through 2010, Waltrip had won at the Bristol Motor Speedway a record 12 times.

Bristol Motor Speedway is one of NASCAR's most popular tracks. It can hold 160,000 fans.

Tennessee's professional football team is the Tennessee Titans. The team moved to Tennessee in 1997 and plays in Nashville's Coliseum. The Titans made it to the Super Bowl in 2000. The Nashville Predators play in the National Hockey League. College sports teams in the state include the Memphis Tigers, the Tennessee Volunteers from Knoxville, and the Vanderbilt Commodores from Nashville.

Miami Dolphins quarterback Chad Pennington played baseball, basketball, and football at the Webb School of Knoxville.

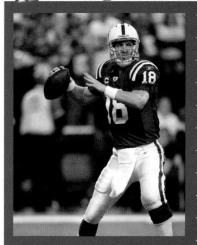

Peyton Manning, quarterback for the Indianapolis Colts, graduated from the University of Tennessee. The school retired his number, 16, in 2005.

Gatlinburg, located at the entrance of Great Smoky Mountains National Park, is one of Tennessee's top snowboarding and skiing locations.

Sportscaster and former Major League Baseball catcher Tim McCarver was born in Memphis in 1941. McCarver attended Christian Brothers High School.

National Averages Comparison

T he United States is a federal republic, consisting of fifty states and the District of Columbia. Alaska and Hawai'i are the only non-contiguous, or non-touching, states in the nation. Today, the United States of America is the third-largest country in the world in population. The United States Census Bureau takes a census, or count of all the people, every ten years. It also regularly collects other kinds of data about the population and the economy. How does Tennessee compare to the national average?

Comparison Chart

United States 2010 Census Data *	USA	Tennessee
Admission to Union	NA	June 1, 1796
Land Area (in square miles)	3,537,438.44	41,217.12
Population Total	308,745,538	6,346,105
Population Density (people per square mile)	87.28	153.97
Population Percentage Change (April 1, 2000, to April 1, 2010)	9.7%	11.5%
White Persons (percent)	72.4%	77.6%
Black Persons (percent)	12.6%	16.7%
American Indian and Alaska Native Persons (percent)	0.9%	0.3%
Asian Persons (percent)	4.8%	1.4%
Native Hawaiian and Other Pacific Islander Persons (percent)	0.2%	0.1%
Some Other Race (percent)	6.2%	2.2%
Persons Reporting Two or More Races (percent)	2.9%	1.7%
Persons of Hispanic or Latino Origin (percent)	16.3%	4.6%
Not of Hispanic or Latino Origin (percent)	83.7%	95.4%
Median Household Income	$52,029	$43,610
Percentage of People Age 25 or Over Who Have Graduated from High School	80.4%	75.9%

*All figures are based on the 2010 United States Census, with the exception of the last two items.

How to Improve My Community

Strong communities make strong states. Think about what features are important in your community. What do you value? Education? Health? Forests? Safety? Beautiful spaces? Government works to help citizens create ideal living conditions that are fair to all by providing services in communities. Consider what changes you could make in your community. How would they improve your state as a whole? Using this concept web as a guide, write a report that outlines the features you think are most important in your community and what improvements could be made. A strong state needs strong communities.

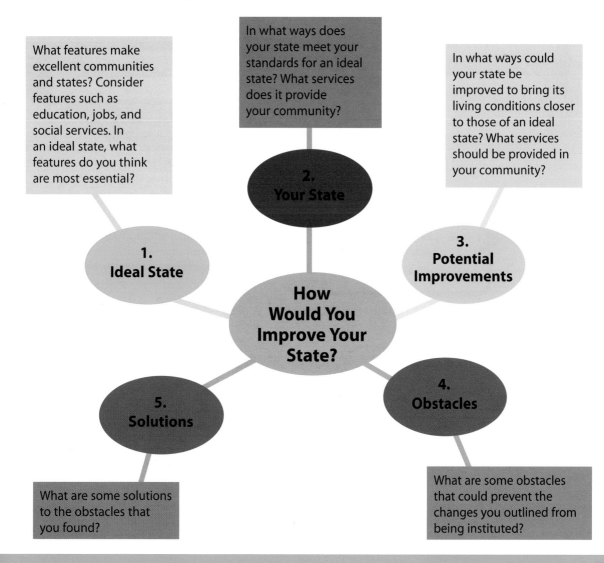

What features make excellent communities and states? Consider features such as education, jobs, and social services. In an ideal state, what features do you think are most essential?

In what ways does your state meet your standards for an ideal state? What services does it provide your community?

In what ways could your state be improved to bring its living conditions closer to those of an ideal state? What services should be provided in your community?

2.
Your State

1.
Ideal State

3.
Potential Improvements

How Would You Improve Your State?

5.
Solutions

4.
Obstacles

What are some solutions to the obstacles that you found?

What are some obstacles that could prevent the changes you outlined from being instituted?

Exercise Your Mind!

Think about these questions and then use your research skills to find the answers and learn more fascinating facts about Tennessee. A teacher, librarian, or parent may be able to help you locate the best sources to use in your research.

1 Which four cities have served as Tennessee's capital?

2 How tall does the state tree, the tulip poplar, grow?

3 True of False? There is a man buried in the Tennessee State Capitol.

4 True of False? Cotton is Tennessee's leading crop.

5 Which U.S. presidents are associated with Tennessee?

6 What is a "Meat and Three"?

7 The town of Shelbyville is known for making which writing tool?

8 How did Maxwell House come up with its company motto, "good to the last drop"?

Words to Know

assassinated: murdered, often for political reasons

ceded: formally surrendered to another

circumference: the outer boundary, especially of a circular area

civil rights movement: the struggle that began in the 1950s and 1960s to provide racial equality for African Americans in the United States

diverse: made up of many different qualities or elements

hydroelectricity: electricity produced by using the power of moving water

industrialized: an economy that is largely based upon manufacturing

municipalities: cities, towns, or villages with their own local government

nocturnal: active at night and inactive during the day

rural: relating to the country

tributaries: streams that flow into larger streams or rivers

Index

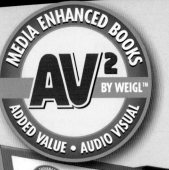

Log on to www.av2books.com

AV² by Weigl brings you media enhanced books that support active learning. Go to www.av2books.com, and enter the special code found on page 2 of this book. You will gain access to enriched and enhanced content that supplements and complements this book. Content includes video, audio, web links, quizzes, a slide show, and activities.

Audio
Listen to sections of the book read aloud.

Video
Watch informative video clips.

Embedded Weblinks
Gain additional information for research.

Try This!
Complete activities and hands-on experiments.

WHAT'S ONLINE?

Try This!	Embedded Weblinks	Video	EXTRA FEATURES
Test your knowledge of the state in a mapping activity.	Discover more attractions in Tennessee.	Watch a video introduction to Tennessee.	**Audio** Listen to sections of the book read aloud.
Find out more about precipitation in your city.	Learn more about the history of the state.	Watch a video about the features of the state.	
Plan what attractions you would like to visit in the state.	Learn the full lyrics of the state song.		**Key Words** Study vocabulary, and complete a matching word activity.
Learn more about the early natural resources of the state.			
Write a biography about a notable resident of Tennessee.			**Slide Show** View images and captions, and prepare a presentation
Complete an educational census activity.			**Quizzes** Test your knowledge.

AV² was built to bridge the gap between print and digital. We encourage you to tell us what you like and what you want to see in the future.

Sign up to be an AV² Ambassador at www.av2books.com/ambassador.